The Coldest Place on Earth

by Kathy Furgang

 HOUGHTON MIFFLIN HARCOURT

PHOTOGRAPHY CREDITS: COVER (bg) ©Ralph Lee Hopkins/National Geographic/Getty Images; 3 (t) ©AridOcean/Shutterstock; 4 (t) ©Ralph Lee Hopkins/National Geographic/Getty Images; 6 (b) ©Byron J. Adams/Office of Polar Programs - National Science Foundation; 7 (t) ©Al Baker/Office of Polar Programs - National Science Foundation; 8 (t) ©Doug Cheeseman/Peter Arnold/Getty Images; 9 (r) ©Emily Stone/Office of Polar Programs - National Science Foundation; 10 (b) ©Thomas Kokta/Getty Images; 13 (b) ©Pasquale Sorrentino/Science Source/Photo Researchers, Inc.

ISBN: 978-0-544-07366-1

8 9 10 0908 21 20 19 18 17

4500668768   A B C D E F G

Contents

Vocabulary

weather   latitude

climate   climate zone

atmosphere   precipitation

equator

Stretch Vocabulary

angle of incidence

phytoplankton

krill

Introduction

Imagine a place so cold, dry, and windy that people can't survive there without staying in well-protected buildings. The land is covered in ice 98% of the time—ice that can be as thick as 1.6 kilometers (1 mile). Few plants or animals can survive in this place of whipping winds and frosty air, where temperatures can dive to more than −80 °Celsius (°C), or −120 °Fahrenheit (°F). And yet this frozen place is considered a desert because there is so little precipitation there.

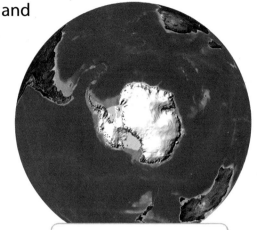

The South Pole is located in Antarctica, a continent in the Southern Ocean.

Is there really a place on Earth with such harsh conditions? Yes! The place is Antarctica, the southernmost continent. Before 1820, no human was known to have set foot there to explore. Since then, the few humans who have traveled there to live are mainly scientists interested in learning more about this harsh ecosystem. What scientists learn in Antarctica can help them better understand the varieties of weather and climate found all over Earth.

Colder Than an Ice Cube

Antarctica is one of Earth's seven continents. It is almost 1.5 times larger than the United States. The region has areas with rugged mountain ranges that rise as high as 5,000 meters (16,000 feet). Along Antarctica's coast are huge platforms of thick, floating ice called ice shelves. More than 40% of Antarctica's coastline is covered in these ice shelves. Few animals live in Antarctica. You may find penguins and seals near the coastline, but few animals can live far inland on the continent's harsh terrain.

The temperature in Antarctica has been known to reach −89 °C (−129 °F). But what makes Antarctica such a cold place? The continual pattern of cold weather forms conditions that keep the area nearly freezing all the time. Remember that weather is the daily change of the conditions of the atmosphere. In Antarctica, it may be snowy one day and windy the next day. Climate is the constant pattern of weather over a long time. The climate of Antarctica is cold and dry.

Distance from the equator affects an area's climate. Areas near the equator have very warm climates. Areas farthest from the equator have very cold climates. The North and South Poles are the points farthest from the equator. The South Pole is located in Antarctica.

The word *latitude* is used to describe a place's distance from the equator. Areas farthest from the equator are described as having a high latitude. Latitudes help divide Earth into different climate zones. Climate zones share similar weather patterns, such as temperature and amount of precipitation. The areas near the poles are called polar zones. Temperatures in the polar zones are extremely cold.

Areas of high latitude are cold because of the way light from the sun strikes Earth's surface. Earth is tilted on its axis. This causes sunlight to hit different parts of Earth at different angles. Sunlight strikes areas in the poles at a lower angle than areas near the equator. The angle at which a line or ray hits a surface is called an angle of incidence. At a low angle of incidence, the sun's solar energy is spread over a large area. The amount of energy that each area receives from sunlight is less than at higher angles. As Earth orbits the sun during one year, angles of incidence change.

Dry as a Bone

When you hear the word *desert*, you probably think of a very hot place with sand and not much else. So, how can cold and icy Antarctica be a desert?

For an area to be considered a desert, it must receive 23 centimeters (10 inches) of precipitation or less each year and have a sandy surface with few plants. Antarctica is actually one of the driest places on Earth, receiving less than 5 centimeters (2 inches) of precipitation each year. Beneath the ice and snow, Antarctica is sandy and barren. Plants are rare in Antarctica because the frozen ground prevents plant roots from breaking through.

Precipitation occurs when water vapor condenses into clouds and then falls. But cold air can't hold as much water vapor as warm air. The air in Antarctica simply cannot hold as much water as air in other parts of the world. Antarctica is so dry precisely *because* it is so cold.

Most of the dry, rocky, sandy surface of Antarctica is covered in ice and snow, which stays on the ground without melting.

Research stations in Antarctica take a battering from frequent powerful windstorms.

Antarctica is not just the coldest but also the *windiest* location on the planet. The average wind speed in Antarctica is 80 kilometers (50 miles) per hour. Record-breaking wind gusts have occurred there at more than 321 kilometers (200 miles) per hour. It's not even possible to measure the wind and temperature in certain areas of Antarctica because the areas are so difficult to reach and have such extreme weather.

The icy continent is colder than the ocean water around it. Because of this, air flows from the colder land outward toward the ocean. Air moves from higher pressure areas to lower pressure areas, and colder air sinks down. As a result, Antarctica's high mountains and cold air cause winds to flow quickly downhill. This constant cycle of moving air can make for a very windy climate. It also contributes to the low temperatures.

During the summer, penguins and other animals can eat enough food to sustain them through the winter months.

It's Summertime!

Antarctica has only two seasons—summer and winter. Each season lasts for six months. Summer in the South Pole is a time of daylight. Earth is tilted on its axis, and the South Pole is facing toward the sun. In winter, the continent gets six months of darkness because it faces away from the sun.

Average summer temperatures in Antarctica are around −7 °C (20 °F). In Antarctica, it's just warm enough for some wildlife to survive in the coastal areas.

The extra hours of daylight make summer a busy time of year. Tiny plant-like organisms called phytoplankton can grow quickly in the nearby ocean water. The phytoplankton provide food for huge populations of krill, tiny sea animals that are food for some marine animals near the shoreline such as seals, penguins, and some kinds of whales.

Summer is also a time when scientists are able to explore the region to learn more about it. In summer, there may be as many as 4,000 people on the continent, while in winter, there are only about 1,000 people. At research posts, scientists use tools for measuring temperature, wind speed, and precipitation.

Scientists are particularly interested in studying Antarctica's ice sheets. During the summer, scientists can take deep core samples of these sheets. Like layers of rock that hold fossils in other climates, Antarctica's ice layers give clues to the past. Each layer has dust, gases, and water that can be uncovered and studied.

Ice core samples can only be collected during Antarctica's summer.

There is certainly a lot of ice to uncover. The Antarctic ice sheet is the world's largest single mass of ice on Earth. Over 14 million square kilometers (5 million square miles) in some areas, the ice sheet extends more than 2,500 meters (8,200 feet) below sea level.

Watch Out for Winter!

When summer is over, the cold, long winter in Antarctica begins. For six months, sunlight doesn't reach this remote corner of Earth for very long. Around June 21, which is the middle of winter in Antarctica, the sun does not rise at all. Antarctica is in complete darkness. That's because the Southern Hemisphere is tilted away from the sun. The latitude of Antarctica is too high for the sun to reach the horizon of this cold area.

As the winter goes on, different locations in Antarctica receive different amounts of sunlight and darkness. At the exact location of the South Pole, this total darkness will last for several months. Areas closer to the coastline have a slightly lower latitude. From these areas, it may be possible to see a sunrise and a sunset during some winter weeks. However, the sun still does not rise very high in the sky.

During the Antarctic winter, coastal areas may have sunrises and sunsets for some weeks, but the South Pole remains in total darkness.

Because sunlight is an important factor in climate, Antarctica's long winters have a major effect on the area's climate.

Only a few animals can survive through winters with little to no sunlight and average temperatures of about −34 °C (−30 °F). It can be especially hard for these animals when temperatures drop to record cold temperatures, such as −89 °C (−129 °F).

The phytoplankton that grow so well in the Antarctic summer continue to provide food for animals in winter. One kind of phytoplankton, algae, becomes trapped in the ice as the temperatures plunge. Algae are plant-like organisms that live in the ocean. Algae drifts near the shoreline and also grows underneath the ice. The algae under the ice becomes a place for krill to gather together during winter to find food and stay alive during the cold, dark months.

The breeding grounds of emperor penguins are near the shoreline in summer, when ice sheets cover a smaller area. With the approach of winter, though, increasing areas of ice place the breeding grounds farther away from the sea. The penguins lay their eggs in winter, so they must travel a distance across the ice to reach their now-inland breeding grounds. The babies hatch as summer approaches, when the ice has melted enough to bring the breeding grounds closer to the coastline—and to a food supply.

Clues in the Ice

Scientists use weather tools to track weather changes in Antarctica. The wind speed, wind direction, air temperature, ocean temperature, and precipitation are tracked and, over time, can be used to collect climate data.

The deepest ice sample is from a level that corresponds to 740,000 years ago. Samples at this level show that Earth's climate was much colder than today, and that it has gone through at least five separate periods of very cold conditions, called ice ages.

Ice samples from levels at 73,000 years ago have a lot of volcanic dust and ash in them. This is evidence of a large volcano that erupted in Indonesia, in which dust and ash blocked out the sun. Evidence of this eruption is found in rock layers around the world, and also in the same layer of ice in Antarctica.

Ice samples from levels at about 12,000 years ago indicate that temperatures dropped very quickly and climates became very cold for another thousand years. High concentrations of salt show times of stormier seas and cooler temperatures.

The amounts of carbon dioxide and other gases in ice samples from levels of recent years can be used to compare our current atmosphere with the atmosphere of the past.

Ice core samples from the 1960s show that there were more radioactive gases in the air before atomic bomb testing was banned. Samples from the late 1980s show a lower concentration of lead after lead-free gasoline was introduced around the world.

Scientists use information they gather about the changing atmosphere to make predictions about the future. Scientists have found that the amount of ice on Antarctic ice shelves has been slowly melting away during summers. However, these changes are very slow, and much slower than in areas closer to the North Pole, such as Greenland.

Antarctica will remain the harshest, coldest, windiest place on the planet for thousands of years to come.

The weather and climate of Antarctica help scientists gather information about conditions around the world.

Make Comparisons

Choose a climate zone other than Antarctica. Research that area's weather and climate, then compare what you find to what you learned about Antarctica. Make a Venn diagram to compare the information about weather and climate in these two separate climate zones.

Write a Travel Brochure

Using the information from this book, make a travel brochure to convince research scientists to work in Antarctica and study the conditions there. Explain why the area is an interesting place to study and what questions scientists would be able to explore on their visit.

Glossary

angle of incidence [AN·gul uv IN·suh·dens] An angle that one straight line makes with a surface.

atmosphere [AT·muh·sfeer] The mixture of gases that surrounds Earth.

climate [KLY·muht] The pattern of weather an area experiences over a long period of time.

climate zone [KLY·muht ZOHN] An area that has similar average temperatures and precipitation throughout.

equator [ee·KWAY·ter] An imaginary line around Earth, equally distant from the North and South Poles.

krill [KRIL] A small, shrimp-like organism that is the main food supply of many marine animals.

latitude [LAT·ih·tood] A measure of how far north or south a place is from the equator.

phytoplankton [FY·toh·plahnk·tuhn] Tiny plant-like organisms that float in the ocean. Most are microscopic.

precipitation [pree·sip·uh·TAY·shuhn] Water that falls from clouds to Earth's surface.

weather [WETH·er] The condition of the atmosphere at a certain place and time.